Our Train Trip

Learning to Add Times by the Half Hour

Mary Ann Thomas

Math
for the
REAL World™

Rosen Classroom Books & Materials
New York

9:30

We are going on a train trip to the city.

We leave our house at 9:30.

It takes a **half hour** to get to the **train station**. There are 30 minutes in a half hour. We get there at 10:00.

10:00   10:30

The next train **arrives** soon. It leaves the train station at 10:30.

10:30   11:00

We ride on the train for a half hour. The train stops at 11:00. People get off and on the train.

11:00   11:30

We stay on the train and ride for 30 more minutes. The train gets to the city at 11:30.

11:30   12:00

It takes us a half hour to walk from the train station to the bookstore. On the way we see many people and big buildings.

We get to the bookstore at 12:00. We stay there for 30 minutes.

12:30   1:00

At 12:30 we take a cab to a place to eat. The ride takes a half hour. We get there at 1:00.

5:00

After lunch, we go shopping. At 5:00 we arrive at the train station to catch our train.

5:00   5:30

We hope to visit the city again soon. Our train leaves in a half hour. What time will that be?

Glossary

arrive (uh-RIVE) To come to a place.

half hour (HAF OUR) Thirty minutes.

train station (TRAYN STAY-shun) A place where trains stop to pick people up and drop them off.